Published in the United States of America by Palmar Press.

First Edition, 2011, 2012

Publisher's Cataloging-in-Publication data
Stewart, Lori Scott.
If I Had As Many Grandchildren As You....! SUMMARY:
Advice in rhyme for grandparents on ways to spark the
imagination of grandchildren - places to go, wonders to see
and fanciful, uplifting things to do.

1. Title, TXu 1-734-260   January 1, 2011

ISBN: 978-0-9839293-0-7 (hardcover)
1. Stories in Rhyme. 2. Wit and Humor. 3. Advice – Fic-
tion. 4. Parenting Advice. 5. Children. 6. Grandparents,
Seniors.

www.ifihadasmanygrandchrenasyou.com

For grandparents everywhere, for you are the memory makers.

There I was sitting outside in my chair,

Just reading my book and breathing fresh air.

When out of the side of my eye I could see

A gaggle of grandchildren heading toward me,

Laughing and skipping all over the place

With great expectations on everyone's face!

I'd promised a plan for adventure and fun,

And thought as I ought, but had not thought of one!

"The Thinker" bronze and marble sculpture by Auguste Rodin

Just then from the garden I heard a low roar,

So I stealthily snuck down the path to explore!

And there big as life and as bold as you please

Was a shaggy maned lion... right there in my peas!

He wore an old cap and a big floppy grin,

And had furry grand paws on which rested his chin!

"What is your name sir?" I yelled in his ear.

"Where did you come from, and why are you here?"

He blinked his brown eyes and then raised his great head,

And glared at me straight through my vegetable bed!

His mouth opened wide as he waggled his tongue,

"My name is Grand Paws and I speak for the young!

The young are quite restless and eager to grow,

To learn of this life and the places they'll go!"

He took a deep breath and then licked his great chops,

"And it's your job to show them 'cause you are their pops!

So I'll tell you this once or quite possibly twice,

That I'm here to impart some sage lion advice

On a few of the things I'd assuredly do,

If I had as many grandchildren as you."

"If I had as many grandchildren as you,

Like seven or nine or eleventy two,

I'd make them my posse, my tribe and my crew,

And gather them up and then here's what we'd do."

"We'd pack buckets and shovels and walk hand in hand

To the beach, where we'd build great huge castles of sand,

With ramparts and turrets and tall drippy towers,

Surrounded by moats filled with boatloads of flowers;

Adorned with pink seashells and beach glass and kelp,

And every last grandchild would pitch in and help!

We'd build roads and tunnels and bridges galore;

Parks, pools and playgrounds, and one ice-cream store!

Mermaids and dragons would guard the great gate

Of this sand-tastic polis - OUR OWN CITY-STATE!"

"Now a sand city-state might just make a nice home,

But grandchild explorers need places to roam.

So I'd round up the herd and we'd gallop and trot

Up the beach to where logs pile up in one spot.

We'd find some old driftwood and build a huge horse,

200 hundred hands high...and so long that of course

All the children could climb on his back for a ride

Down the beach, on the wind, through the waves at low tide!

And of course if we added a couple of things

Like a straight spiraled horn and a new set of wings,

With a magical leap we could take to the sky...

High up to the clouds where the unicorns fly!"

Driftwood Horses by Heather Jansch and Jack Marsden-Meyer /PS

O'er sparkling blue oceans we'd fly like the 'cirque'

To pride lands where tricksters and wild things lurk.

We'd soar the savannah in hot air balloons,

And sleep in tree tents that hang down like cocoons.

We'd wing with crowned cranes to Victoria Falls.

O'er pyramids, temples and China's great walls;

Across Persian deserts, up high mountain heights

To icecaps and glaciers, where bright northern lights

Would shimmer and dance to the music of spheres.

Such sights will turn kids into IMAGINEERS!

Hot Air Balloon Kenya, Africa

Portaledge with mosquito netting in Monterey Cypress

Great Wall of China between Simatai and Jinshanling

Great Pyramids at Giza, Egypt

Persepolis, one of the four capitals of ancient Persia, now Iran

Northern Lights over Tombstone Territory Park, Yukon

"Sparked and inspired and totally beat,

It's time to head home and get something to eat!

Colorful popovers filled with plum jam,

Bright turkey pancakes with scrapple and ham,

Fluffernut sandwiches, bread a la boeuf...

A feast that at least should be served... on the ROOF!"

"After some cookies and pink lemonade,

We'd dress up in costumes and start a ...PARADE!

Our costumes are not something bought off the shelves.

We'd find some old fabric and make them ourselves!

We'd gather fake fur and some tall wooden stilts,

Strong thread, beads and feathers and African quilts,

Some paper mache and bright paint to make masks,

And in no time at all, we would finish our tasks!

And to our amazement the costumes we'd made,

Would be just the thing for a WILDLIFE PARADE!!!!"

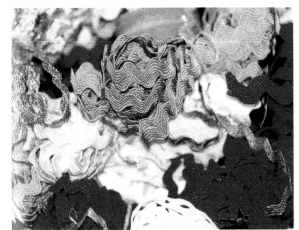

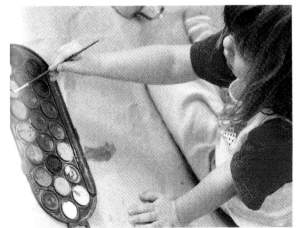

"Meercats and warthogs and laughing hyenas,

And zebras and cheetahs, but none quite as keen as

The graceful giraffe loping by on tall stilts,

And the leaping gazelle in her plaid Scottish kilts!

White rhinos and hippos, bright scarlet macaws,

And a big shaggy lion with furry grand paws!

We'd parade through the poppy fields up to the trees,

Where grandkids could sing just as loud as they please!

The voices of children would ring into space,

Until kingdom came to that glorious place!"

"The Lion King" Musical - Circle of Life

"I wouldn't stop there...there's much more I would do,

If I had as many grandchildren as you!

I'd teach them to work, and to play and to pray ~

A little of each, and a little each day.

We'd learn to fix floor boards and doors when they squeak,

Old toys that are broken, and chimneys that leak.

I'd read them all stories and teach them to fish,

And give them all stars upon which they could wish!"

"I'd hang presents and popcorn and candy from trees,

so grandkids could pick them whenever they please!

We'd race around chasing big dreams and small bugs,

Then gather around for a round of group hugs!

We'd search every sunset for flashes of green,

And upside down rainbows would often be seen...

Smiling beguilingly down from the sky,

As we laze in the grass watching clouds floating by!

Now lazing is something we'd not often do,

But sometimes we would... if we could! Wouldn't you?"

Green flash phenomena seen at sunset, just as the sun dips below the horizon

Sunlight hitting hexagonal ice crystals create a 'circumzenithal arc' - upside down rainbow!

"With our heads full of bugs and green grass in our hair,

Ideas would start popping right out of thin air!

We'd build a small village of tiny moss homes,

For magical creatures like fairies and gnomes;

Float flickering candles across the night lake;

Watch moonsets and sunrises right at day break!

Sometimes we'd just want to do a good deed

With our walloping driftwoody unicorn steed,

Hitched to the front of a beach buggy sleigh

Filled with old toys that we'd hidden away.

We'd race through the hills full of toy gifts galore,

And give them to kids who would play with them more."

Woodland Fairy House

Beach Fairy House

"Of course I would teach them to sing and to dance.

And then I would give them a wonderful chance

To move people more than they'd ever thought,

By thoughtfully using the talents they've got!

We'd transport the troupe to a grand central station

To dance in an impromptu flash mob formation!

The sweet sounds of music would loudly be blaring;

The whole weary world would stop and start staring

At grandchildren dancing and laughing and caring.

And thus would they learn that this life is for sharing!

Those are but a few of the things I would do,

If I had as many grandchildren as you!"

Flash Mob for UNICEF Convention on the Rights of the Child in Havana

Eurovision Flash Mob Dance

Photo Credits in Order of Appearance

ROOSEVELT PUBLIC LIBRARY
27 WEST FULTON AVENUE
ROOSEVELT NY 11575
516-378-0222

04/19/2013